When Auntie Died

Death Through the Lens of a Child

By Eileen L. Tapper
Mental Health Therapist

Bean Station, Tennessee, USA
All Rights Reserved.

ISBN 978-0-9791558-2-6

© 2024 Eileen L. Tapper
—Revised Edition—

Illustrator: Donna Ellery
Stowe, Vermont

All rights reserved, including the right of reproduction in any form, or by any mechanical or electronic means including photocopying or recording, or by any information storage or retrieval system, in whole or in part in any form, and in any case not without the written permission of the author and publisher.

Printed in the United States of America
Distributed Worldwide

Dedication

To my sister who died during the pandemic, changing the way children grieve, and to my daughter, in whom those changes were captured.

When Auntie died,
I couldn't breathe.

My eyes filled with tears,
and my breath disappeared.

My body shivered, and my stomach felt like it would hurt for years.

This happened to me when Auntie died.

When Auntie died, I didn't get to say "Good-Bye."
Just one more time, I wanted a hug.
To feel her squeeze me and hold me close.

To run to her when Mommy dropped me off. When Auntie died, I didn't get to say

"Good-Bye."

"It can't be true!" I cried.

"I don't believe I'll never see her again!" I argued.

"Where did she go?" I asked.

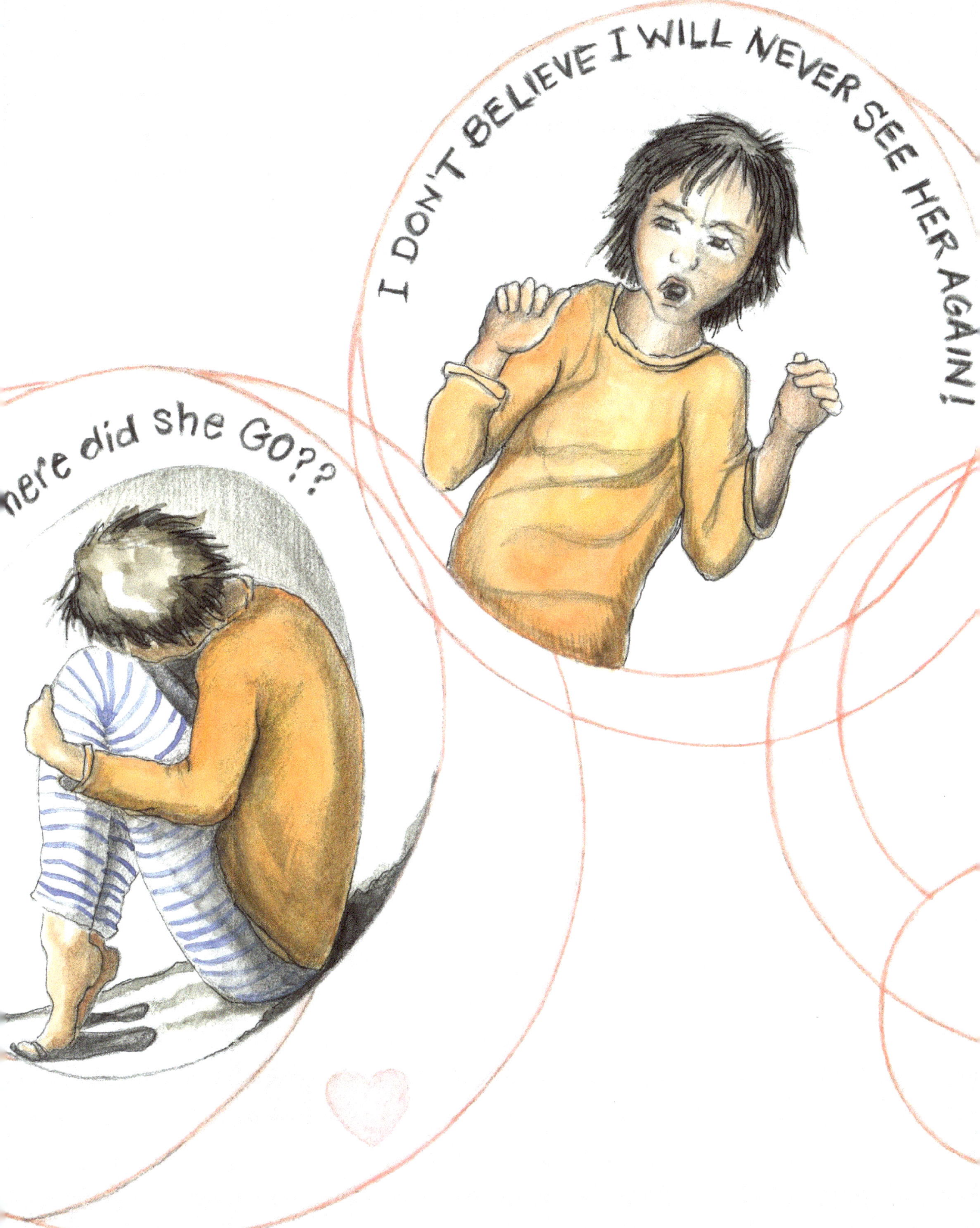

I DON'T BELIEVE I WILL NEVER SEE HER AGAIN!
nere did she GO??

"Is she OK?" I wondered.

"Is she sad, like me?" I thought.

When Auntie died, I couldn't think about her. It broke my heart and gave me feelings I didn't want to feel.

"Don't say her name!" I pleaded.

"Please, don't talk about her," I cried.

I ran to my room. I turned up my music.

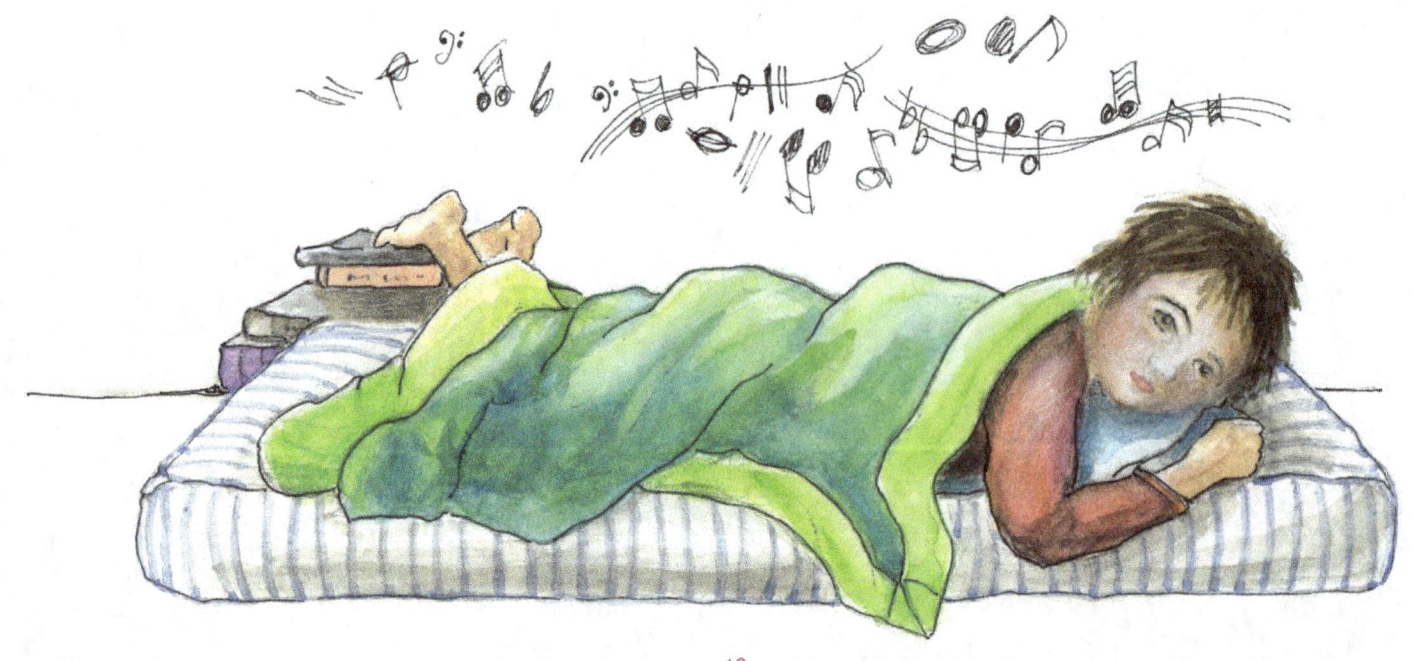

I swung on my swing, very high, for hours.

I tried to escape, but there was no place to hide when Auntie died.

Mommy held me close.
We cried together.
We remembered my Auntie,
and we missed her
the same.
Mommy hurt too!
Not even Mommy
got to say "Good-Bye."
We both felt sad.

When Auntie died.

One day, Mommy told me she spoke to my Auntie the day *before* she died. And Mommy giggled! She remembered how Auntie made us laugh!

How my Auntie asked for peaches and sweet tea the day *before* she died.

Mommy told me she called the nurses at the hospital to get my Auntie peaches and sweet tea.
"And hurry!" she said.

Because the pandemic kept us away. "Sweet tea and peaches!" my Auntie wanted. The day *before* she died.

We shared other stories, what we each remembered. Who my Auntie was and the things we did together, *before* my Auntie died.

Mommy told me about my Great Grandmother, who always made Red Rose® tea, and how she and my Auntie drank it to remembered her.

So, we also made Red Rose® tea, and drank it together, to remember my Auntie.

That same day,
we shopped for a
peach tree, and found one
with a single peach.

It was perfect!

I believed that peach held
the spirit of my Auntie.

We planted it in her
special spot on the lawn,
where my Auntie sat to
watch me play.

And when I felt sadness creep over me,
I went to talk to my Auntie,
a single peach, on her special tree,
and I felt her in my life again.

Spring came, and new leaves filled my Auntie's tree.

The branches grew thicker, and the leaves grew fuller.

The tree grew stronger, and the trunk grew wider.

The lone peach was gone but the memories were still there.
And the stories, like the peach tree, reminded me of my Auntie.

We will always miss my Auntie,
but the stories keep her close.
Our stories, when my Auntie was alive.
And even though our hearts feel sad,
sometimes...remembering her
lifts us up and makes us giggle.

I LOVE YOU

Because she was the best Auntie in the whole wide world, and I got to have time with her when she was alive, *before* my Auntie died.

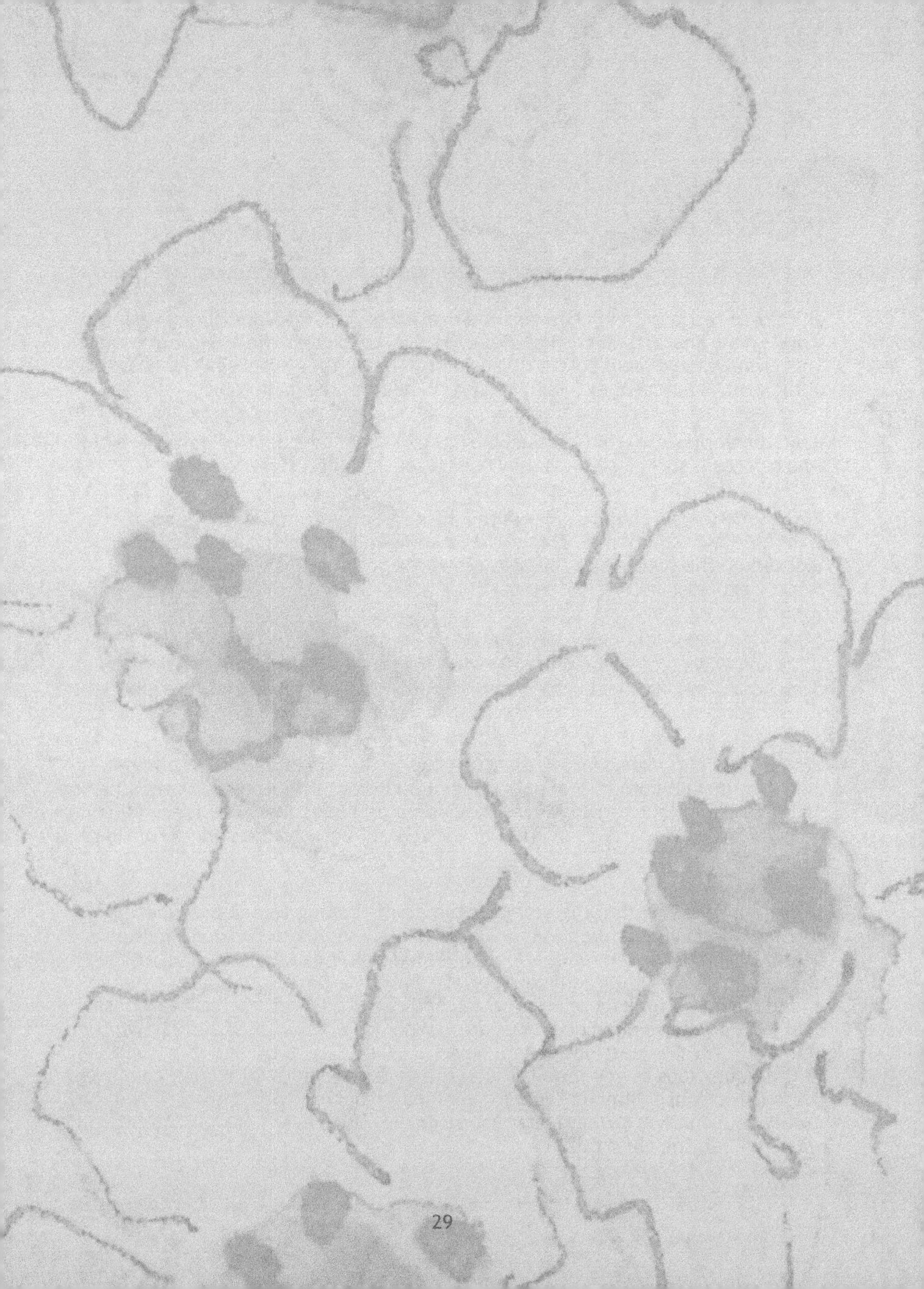

Reader's Guide

This story is called a bibliotherapy—a book that has a therapeutic effect on those who read it. The purpose of a bibliotherapy is to elicit a strong, intense, emotional response, which begins the healing process. By identifying with the story's main characters, the listener can begin to express their own experiences. This creates movement forward, thus normalizing the responses and reactions of the central theme of events. In this story, death is the main topic.

Read the entire story to the child who has experienced a death event. For a child who can read, stay close by as they read it, or share the story together.

Allow time for the child to process the information within the story and relate it to their own experience. This could be immediate or take a few days. Stay focused on the purpose of this story towards processing their unique grief-related expressions.

Observe the child for signs and symptoms of distress. Encourage healthy coping skills and ways to seek comfort. Provide for these needs as they arise. Yoga, deep breathing, blowing bubbles, bubble baths, nature walks, etc., are excellent stress reducers.

How is the child experiencing their feelings within the body? What body language do you notice? Any physical complaints or symptoms? Are they having nightmares or night terrors? Have they asked any questions? Are there clinging behaviors or new fears? Be mindful of these reactions and the severity of them. Take notes.

There are pauses within the story for the adult reading to a child, where probing questions could be asked. These pages are marked with a small pink heart. Upon the second read, ask open-ended probing questions to assist the child in processing their individual grief-related responses to death. Open-ended questions seek more information and remove a "yes" or "no" response. Examples of open-ended questions are: "Who do we know that died?" "What do you feel?" "What questions do you have?" "What do you think death means?" Ask the questions as you read through the pages and allow the story to elicit a personal response. Stay on topic for each page marked with a heart. "Tell me more about that" or "What I hear you saying is...Do I have that right?" are good ways to keep the child talking.

Label emotions and feelings. Discuss how the body expresses these. Allow the child to share their thoughts, emotions, and feelings about their own death experience.

Be direct, honest, and use terms that are concrete and clear. Avoid words like; lost, sleeping, gone, went to heaven, etc., as the child may look for the person who died and not understand. Avoid fantasy or obscure, abstract concepts. Avoid relating death to religious beliefs or principles of faith. Teach age-related facts about dying. Ex: Their heart stopped. They no longer breathe. Their body stopped working. Explain how the heart keeps a person alive and when it stops, the person dies.

Use the name of the person who died to make it personal for the child.

Death removes the role of the person who has died. This gap in the child's life must be filled with other ways for this person to continue being an important part of the child's life. How the person lived within the child's life was recounted and retold in the story. These stories are kept alive, which keeps the role active. Stories can be kept alive by re-telling, making a memory book, looking at photos or videos, or having a special place related to the person who died. In the story, the peach tree signifies a replacement role. The tree becomes the place where the child can still talk to the Auntie and share how they feel. It's a living memorial instead of a tombstone. Photos were also used in the story to recount the things the Auntie and child did together.

Traditions are also important in the child's life. Making connections from previous experiences of loved ones who died creates a ritual for death events within the family. In the story, drinking Red Rose® tea was already an important ritual for remembering loved ones who had died. Create a link with something memorable or personable to the person who died and bring that aspect into the child's life.

Never allow the pain of death to block expressing how it feels to experience the death of a loved one. Talk about it. Share how it feels. Normalize how intense it can be. Allow the child to realize others feel the same. Make room for death experiences in the child's life so as they grow, they will know how to cope and process their pain.

Know when to seek professional help. When the grief is too far out of reach for you to be of support for your child. When the child is experiencing thoughts or acts that are a danger to themselves or others. When the child shuts down and their personality changes, dramatically. Seek professional help.

www.ingramcontent.com/pod-product-compliance
Lightning Source LLC
Chambersburg PA
CBHW081629100526
44590CB00021B/3660